Learning to Breathe

poems by

Cindy Buchanan

Finishing Line Press
Georgetown, Kentucky

Learning to Breathe

ACKNOWLEDGMENTS

My deepest gratitude to the editors of the following publications, in which
versions of some of these poems first appeared:

"Downtown Tourists;" "No Sunflowers Here" in *Evening Street Review*
"Unacceptable" in *Iris Literary Journal*
"A Gift of Bougainvillea Blossoms" in *Chestnut Review*
"Lamentation" in *The MacGuffin*
"For You, Again" in *Mobius*
"Fear Less;" "This Morning Before Coffee;" "Dear Daughter on the Street of
Dreams" in *Hole in the Head Review*
"Listen" in *Streetlight Magazine*
"Recalculating" in *The Write Launch*

Publisher: Leah Huete de Maines
Editor: Christen Kincaid
Cover Art: Brenton Buchanan
Author Photo: Scott Buchanan
Cover Design: Elizabeth Maines McCleavy

Order online: www.finishinglinepress.com
also available on amazon.com

Author inquiries and mail orders:
Finishing Line Press
PO Box 1626
Georgetown, Kentucky 40324
USA

Table of Contents

for my family

love letter from your mother

can you recognize
me
where i stand
half-buried
amid the blades
of sharp beach grass
the cold wind hurling
promises made
across years

i reach deep
into my shadows
to pull out
these pages
leaden with letters
whose cold
black edges
flay you
with love

Downtown Tourists

I thought
I saw you today
slumped against the shaded wall
of a downtown department store.

Your backpack was tossed carelessly
on the concrete sidewalk.
You (not you) moved carefully
to nurse a tiny open flame

that caught my attention.
Not your rail-thin crumpled body.
Too common.
But the flame, in the middle of a hot August day

over which, trembling,
you held a piece of blackened tin foil.
I tried not to look
but the syringe in your lap drew me in.

Across the street,
waiting for the walk signal to change,
stood a family of four.
Summer tourists.

Skin smooth, hair trimmed, clothes clean.
Two parents, two teenagers.
One girl, one boy.
So young, innocent like you were once.

I wanted to warn them: avert your eyes.
Or, look closely.
This too, even you,
Could be.

Why

No, she didn't have an accident.
No, she wasn't prescribed oxy for an injury.
No, she didn't come from a broken home.
No, neither parent suffered an illness, died,
was incarcerated, was an addict, was abusive.
No, no sexual abuse. No rape. No violation.
No, she wasn't diagnosed with learning disabilities,
or bipolar disorder, or schizophrenia.
No, she was a happy child.
She didn't do well in high school,
though, never found her place.
No, we loved her.
Her brother and her aunts
and her uncles and her grandparents
all loved her, told her that they
loved her, showed her they loved her.
No, I didn't recognize the warning signs.
Yes, I should have done more.
No, I don't know anything more.
I asked. I asked. I asked.
I asked. I asked.
I ask.

Unacceptable

What made her feel she didn't
belong, made her howl for approval,
blinded her to love?

When she scarred her skin,
razored it with pain,
did it numb her ache?

Does she regret
the ring she stole, the lies
she told, the times she ran away?

The time she tried to forget to breathe?

Is she still hooked on smack,
on crystal too? Do they ease
her cravings?

And does she still mourn her unborn,
whisper lullabies in empty rooms
when she thinks no one can hear?

How do you cry a prayer?

Does she ever feel she can
walk into an embrace and be felt,
seen, heard, known as sacred?

Without belonging, souls become weightless.
Without belonging, souls fade, dissipate
like an exhalation on a frosty winter morning.

A Gift of Bougainvillea Blossoms

This latest gift weighs dark,
heavy as a low cloud drooping with rain.
The leafy bracts are creased sharp.
The colors run wound-red to bruise-purple.

I hold the blossoms in my outstretched hand,
searching for words tattooed upon the petals,
assaying for flattery, criticism, blame—
measuring this gift against others of its kind.

I refuse to bring the flowers close or find
their scent. Acceptance might unbalance me,
dispel the bitter taste of iron upon my tongue.
I have spent years perfecting my response

but I am tired. Death is taking form,
drumming her fingers upon my chest.
My hand trembles. I let go and am
astonished when the bougainvillea float

softly to the ground, light as hummingbird wings.
They are flowers, nothing more, exquisite
and fragile for a second. I pick one up,
and cradle the blossom in the palms of my hands.

Lamentation

Addiction darkens the early hours of the morning
bringing me to solitary grief, invisible in my mourning.

Curse the scourge of heroin and methamphetamine,
demons that diminish my daughter, deny me this morning.

Even the rising sun whose rays caress the windowpane
fails before it reaches me. For her, I am in mourning.

God toys with us, dangles "daughter" on a chain,
holds her between life and death in my mind this morning.

I wear blame like prison garb, continue to maintain
jurors would find me guilty. I sentence myself to mourning.

Keening, I repent of errors made that stain
love and leave me yearning for her each morning.

Mothers like me tally their transgressions, paint
numerous vignettes of opportunities lost, insist on mourning.

Over years, hope erodes like a mountain washed with rain.
Prayer becomes stuck as if frozen by a winter morning.

Queries (how are you? where are you?) again and again
result in lies and more lies. They spiral me deeper into mourning.

Sometimes she surfaces suddenly like a fast-moving hurricane,
tempestuous and turbulent, as if to regain every lost morning.

Until she disappears again, her energy spent, her intent drained,
veins crying in complaint—for their dark nourishment, mourning.

When, finally, from my bed I rise, I inhale all the possibility of pain,
exhale the possibilities of life, breathe so I can meet the morning.

You might say I'm blind to hope (addicted to shame), that I'm a zealot whose name begins with sin. But this is my mourning.

Somewhere Else

Somewhere else
there is a woman
staring out her window too

We see not
the locust trees or snow
nor the blinding blue of sky

but the replay
of the way we stroked
a face—or didn't

and I want to ask her
if we will ever find
our way to now

and how do we
unfilm our mind

see the silver weight
of water in the bay

hear blush pink geraniums
awake in spring

feel silence

in the swoop of a Great Horned Owl

After the Hose to the Washer Burst

after the valve was closed
and the floors warped,
I was left
to sift through all that had accumulated
out of sight
behind what I assumed
would function indefinitely.

I found yellow dog hair and wads
of wet lint, coins, slippery with slime,
hair bands and ink-smeared receipts,
a shattered Bic pen,
your pink polka-dotted ankle sock
with three tiny plastic baggies still in the toe,
and a key to the house from before

I changed the locks
after my watch and gold earrings
ended up at the local pawn shop, after
you, dear girl, punctured my veins.
In this empty,
I learn to replace valves, repair broken
hoses, walk on warped floors

Fear Less
with gratitude to Pema Chodron

This morning when I stepped onto the familiar path,
the wild north wind
met me with her sleeted breath, stung my eyes,
numbed my ears, promised

me stories uncomfortable, unwanted. I howled back,
believing her, pushed
myself against her too—without effect—until I shifted

opened wide my arms and bid the wind climb in so I might trace
her hidden face, soothe and call her by my name, and offer

a different story: thanks for her sure song
thanks for coming one more day.

Dear Hungry Ghost

The day you hitched a ride
out of my life and into an alien world

my knees shattered the floorboards.
I had been taught to pray past despair

as if prayer was currency, and hope
could be bought with a wallet

filled with supplications. I offered pleas,
stacked them until they reached

from foundation to the roof and still
I could not buy you back. Spent, I stood,

bowed to the unfathomable, and took
one deep breath for me, then one for you.

No exchange of anything: breath releasing
me and you, my beloved hungry ghost.

No Sunflowers Here

Just beyond the glass doors, my planter
boxes lie end to end across the balcony.
They are six feet long, one foot wide—
narrower than me, although I am shrinking now,
diminishing bit by bit. The blossoms thrive
with daily watering and the heat of my hands
as I prune leaves, gauge the dampness of the soil.

Blushing geraniums are the divas of my garden.
The Calla lilies pretend to purity like priests
in white surplices. I use the purple lavender
for sachets, and the green mint for simple pleasures:
posies, tea, coolness on the tongue. The weeds
I leave for when I need to feel the power
of destruction. I did not plant sunflowers.

Sunflowers spiral too much with perfection,
their seeds arrayed in a hypnotic, intentional
design. Each seed is both male and female,
sufficient unto itself. Each seed is tucked tightly
to the next at a perfect golden angle in a pattern
so precisely sequenced it denies the probability
of chance, suggests there's something more.

When one seed from the sunflower fails,
the perfection is broken. Such a reminder
of promise (and loss) would be too much,
especially on those days when I turn to face
the sun but find it missing. So I make do
with geraniums, lavender, Callas, mint,
and weeds that hold no mystery, though I admit
the sunflower is conspicuous in its absence.

For You, Again

What would you say
if I told you
I see your face
when I avoid the eyes
of a woman begging for change
on the street corner
and when I return to press
some crumpled bills into her
outstretched hand?

At the shelter for homeless women,
I stand behind
the lunch counter
offering spoonfuls
of donated food
to the smiling, unsmiling,
battered, crazy, addicted
hapless and hopeful
young and old.

One day, a young woman
—blonde ponytail, blue eyes—
(blackened and missing teeth,
tattoos sliding out of her sleeves
and creeping above the neckline
of her misbuttoned blouse)
appeared at the counter,
and I had to turn from not you
and not call her by your name.

I'd hoped to not hope
to see you there.
The stories I tell myself
about your life
are rich in detail
but short on facts.

I imagine you everywhere
and nowhere I would
wish you to be.

This Morning Before Coffee

I catch the Calla Lilies lifting
their creamy bracts to the first
filaments of dawn, a silent
private act of reverence, adoration.
Outlined against the steel-gray sky,
they stand erect and still, trumpet-
throated, waiting for a sign to praise
with psalms the promises of day

—or are they performing an act of
supplication: slender Calla stems
thrusting open spathes toward heaven
so their golden tongues might decry
the fragility of their pale flesh, mourn
how easily torn and broken
they can be, and plead for intervention,
a commutation that halts their slow decay?

A puff of wind interrupts my reveries.
The lilies resume their stoic roles
of sentries in the window box. I see
the difference between praise and supplication
is moot; both are lonely cries flung upward
to what is forever mute. Is it wise to emulate
the lilies? The dirt, after all, welcomes every
thing, each one, regardless, with great tenderness.

Poised at 3 am

Like a black crow on a bare branch
one claw lifted
poised to launch myself
into the repetend of grief

one claw lifted
forced smiles contort my mouth
in the repetend of grief
it is a wonder I can move at all

forced smiles contort my mouth
I listen for the scream of sirens
it is a wonder I can move at all
you are far, too far away

I listen for the scream of sirens
to tell me you overdosed
far, too far away from me
I will be called

to tell me you overdosed
I launch myself into grief
I will be called
a black crow on a bare branch

Listen

When I first conceived of you I was
inside a graffiti-covered phone booth
near a rundown beach motel. I wept.

The OB's voice on the other end
filled with static. You swam through
the phone line anyway, lodged for years

inside my heart before you sped
away. I loved you as best I could,
but leaving was what you got good at—

lured by street meds, accelerating down
tracks that imprisoned us both.
Do you ever pass abandoned booths and

wish you could make one call?
Pick up the phone. Hear
my blood pound in your veins.

Dear Daughter on the Street of Dreams

It's one of those holidays again,
whole days when I pretend
you call
to tell me you're sorry you haven't

because you are
        exhausted from staying up with your crying newborn
because you are
        busy moving into a place of your own, with a bathroom,
        maybe even a bedroom
because you are
        working a new job—the kind, you know, I would be proud of

I decide to clean, and in a chipped cup in a kitchen drawer
I find
the house key I took
back when I left you at rehab ten years ago.

The locks are changed now—
the key only works to open
a casket of fear
                     dreams
           since you disappeared onto strange streets
                 paved with black tar
                   stained
             with the sweat of forgetting

where the acrid need
to hold you
burns holes in my skin

Recalculating

I'm in my lane, staying between the center line
and the rough gravel on the shoulder,
when Jack White bursts from the radio
screaming *Jo-o-lene* and I'm stabbed in the chest
by the spike of red rage and white pain:
I could never love again.
I hear Jack fall to his knees
like I did when they called to report
you'd ditched rehab and headed west
towards a tar-colored sun. Heroin's
my Jolene and I'm pleading along with Jack:
please
don't take my man, and I want to say
please
don't take my daughter, but that would be
too near—I'd end up in a ditch—
so I yell *man* to keep myself going. It's a pretense,
of course. Sometimes delusion is the only
road forward when you *cannot compete.*
Still, I have to spend the next few miles
recalculating the route to quiet summer meadows,
whole places emptied of red poppies, devoid
of the insistent cries of mourning doves.

How to Pronounce *Grief*

Go ahead. Say it slow
so that it begins
in the throat. You need
to close the muscles
around the sound
as if to trap it there
for as long as you can
before your tongue touches
the softness of your palate,
your voice escapes,
and *grief* begins:
hard *g*, howl of *r*,
then the *eeee* that travels
into your mouth to lodge
between your teeth
and pull your cheeks
in a travesty of a smile.
Your breath flows out,
sends the final *fffff*
across your lips and off
into a space you are still
trying to understand.

Walk with Me

Come, walk with me:
hands open, palms down, outstretched.
Start slowly, skimming the feathered tips
of the tall dried grasses beside the path. Feel how
the stalks shift and bend beneath your hands.

Quicken your pace and move on
to brush prickly rock roses, caress
the blushing curves of ripe rose hips.
See how the dried petals curl and retract.
Even in dying they still cradle the fruit.

Reach out farther and let your palms
slide across smooth aspen bark
scarred with black eyes that see you with me.
Tiny amber teardrops from nearby pines
leave our hands sticky, fragrant.

Then stretch, reach up towards the insubstantial
clouds and taste their dampness, dance through
to hold the waxing moon that floats swollen and lopsided.
Rest there, breathless, palms open. Live
in the moment it takes for the grass to pass under our hands.

Awakening

I run beside the bay, a ritual
to sift through the accumulation of
late night film noir that loops behind my eyes.
The sun streaks pink through early morning clouds
layered above the distant mountain range.
My ragged breath soon smooths to match the beat
of my feet upon the trail. Each inhale,
exhale, takes in, sends out, a low deep thrum
of hymn and prayer. And in these moments
night's dark clouds dissipate, for here is real:
wisps of fog drifting soft above the waves,
the sudden *puff* of a seal, surfacing
and curious, pearls of dew on rosehips,
a wild rabbit, still, underneath a hedge.

Choice

In a dark and silent bower
just before the bridge that crosses
the wide and deep Columbia,
a child's bike, painted white,
leans against a massive tree trunk.
The basket is filled with seasonal
remembrances: small pumpkins
for fall, yellow daffodils in spring,
red-white-blue streamers in the summer.
Winter storms bring snow, crystals
spilling into the pale cold light. And, always,
a small brown teddy bear placed just so
amid the flowers, streamers, snow.

My daughter had a white bear
she carried everywhere—except
to where she lives: now
her dark streets are strewn with needles,
festooned with false promises.
White is the color of sorrow; I am
its gray silhouette. I will not yet
mourn her with cut flowers
or toys or other dead things. I hear
the river, swooshing, pulsing, and
I choose to listen
to the chord of life, choose
the sound of infinite possibility.

With Thanks

Thank you to my talented son, Brenton Buchanan, for the cover art, and to my First Thursday Poetry Group for their encouragement and feedback on the poems in this book.

I am deeply grateful to Anne Boyer, friend and first reader, for her unwavering interest in and support of my poetry. And many thanks to Susan Knox for her generosity in sharing information and writing resources with me. Thanks to the teachers and students at Hugo House for the many inspiring and informative poetry classes. Special thanks to Jeanine Walker and Gabrielle Bates for their guidance and support.

Finally, this book would not have been possible without the loving support of my husband, Scott, whose humor and calmness keeps me sane even in the most chaotic of times.

Cindy Buchanan was raised in Alaska, has a B.A. in English from Gonzaga University, and taught preschool until she retired. She studies poetry at Hugo House in Seattle, Washington where she currently lives, and is a member of two monthly poetry groups. She is a lifelong learner and writer, a (slow) runner and hiker, and a beginning student of Buddhism. Her work has been published in *Chestnut Review, Evening Street Review, The MacGuffin, Hole in the Head Review*, and other journals. Visit her at cindybuchanan.com